Suit Up
PUTTING ON THE FULL ARMOR OF GOD

BEACON HILL PRESS
OF KANSAS CITY

Suit Up
PUTTING ON THE FULL ARMOR OF GOD

Editor
Mike L. Wonch
Director of Curriculum
Merritt J. Nielson
Director of Editorial
Bonnie Perry
Writer
James Matthew Price

Copyright 2014 by Beacon Hill Press of Kansas City

ISBN: 978-0-8341-3141-5
Printed in U.S.A.

10 9 8 7 6 5 4 3 2 1

CONTENTS

The Christian life is not all potluck dinners and hymn-singing. Nobody knew that better than the apostle Paul:

Five times I received from the Jews the forty lashes minus one. Three times I was beaten with rods, once I was pelted with stones, three times I was shipwrecked, I spent a night and a day in the open sea, I have been constantly on the move. I have been in danger from rivers, in danger from bandits, in danger from my fellow Jews, in danger from Gentiles; in danger in the city, in danger in the country, in danger at sea; and in danger from false believers (2 Corinthians 11:24-26).

Today, it's a dangerous world for anyone seriously trying to live for God. As Paul says, "our struggle is not against flesh and blood, but against the rulers, against the authorities, against the powers of this dark world and against the spiritual forces of evil in the heavenly realms" (Ephesians 6:12b). However, God supplies us with everything we need not just to survive, but to win the battle. *Suit Up: Putting on the Full Armor of God* will guide you through God's armory and help you discover how each piece is designed to protect and strengthen your spiritual life.

So get ready. Lace up your boots, strap on your armor, secure your helmet, and see that your weapon is ready. The battle may be rough, but "put on the full armor of God, so that when the day of evil comes, you may be able to stand your ground, and after you have done everything, to stand" (Ephesians 6:13).

Matt Price is the chair of the Christian ministry department at Mount Vernon Nazarene University, where he teaches classes on Christian education and intercultural studies. He has served as a youth pastor, curriculum editor, pastor, and missionary. After living in Kansas City, Cote d'Ivoire, South Africa, France, and Benin, Matt now lives in rural Knox County, Ohio, with his wife and two sons.

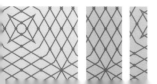

Be Prepared

The Desire for Protection

Protection is a basic human desire. Humans seek safety above all else—we can benefit from neither food nor clothing if our survival is continually threatened. The study of primitive cultures around the world reveals that the first task of human society is to provide security—protection against the elements of nature. Researchers around the globe have found that a society at war cannot be brought to peace by police action and diplomatic sanctions alone—it must also provide basic security for its citizens. Much closer to home, the nesting instinct is one of the strongest human instincts—just ask young parents-to-be. The desire to protect ourselves and what we value most comes from our desire for security, strength, and self-sufficiency.

However, such security can be compared to an infant's pacifier. The pacifier prompts the baby's suckling reflex even though it doesn't give the nourishing milk. The pacifier provides the semblance of what the baby needs, and prompts the appropriate reaction, but the need is not actually met. It is like building a fence for a flock of lambs without noticing the wolf hiding inside the barrier—the threat still remains. The establishment of laws in a nation also depends upon law-abiding citizens—the threat of legal consequences does not always deter the determined criminal. Our pursuit of security does not always provide true protection.

When it comes to spiritual protection, many people believe that Christians are securely positioned in Christ so that nothing will harm them. There is a faith in one's proximity to the Savior as if there is a force field shielding one from the darkness that abounds in the hearts of many in this world. In a way there can never be a fence or wall high enough to guard against every evil scheme.

Believers may, however, find shelter from the swirling tempests of this world. In the laws of the Old Testament, the Israelites were commanded to build shelter in recognition of God's provision of safety during their flee from Egypt, an act celebrated in the Feast of Sukkoth (Leviticus 23; Nehemiah 8). Everlasting shelter, however, comes only through dwelling with God himself, as evidenced in Psalms: "Whoever dwells in the shelter of the Most High will rest in the shadow of the Almighty" (Psalm 91:1; see also 27:5; 55:8; 61:4). God promises this shelter to those who are willing to live faithfully for Him (Psalm 91:14-16).

Reflect on this...

Do you agree or disagree with the author that protection is a basic human desire? Why?

What are some differences between security and the biblical idea of shelter?

According to the psalmist, what are some ways God provides shelter?

The Temptation of Self-Sufficiency

The desire for protection also encourages people to rely on their own strength. The history of Western civilization is filled with examples of modern heroes that apparently needed no outside assistance to succeed. In the 20th century, the heroic stories of self-made scientists like Albert Einstein, daring explorers like the Apollo astronauts, and savvy tech entrepreneurs like Bill Gates continue to create the idyllic notion that people may become what they want to be by their own volition. But as it goes so often with heroic tales, there is more to the story.

Much has been written about these modern heroes, and in every story there is a common theme—each of them needed someone else along their road to success. Bill Gates had Paul Allen, Einstein had the Olympia Academy, and the Apollo astronauts were part of a team of like-minded colleagues that challenged and cajoled each other toward success. These individuals were part of larger movements, though that does not detract from their personal roles in their respective successes. These modern heroes have been individually successful, but they were never alone in reaching their success. The modern American myth of rugged individualism is not completely accurate. It did not take long for the spiritual vacuum of personal success to create a hunger for spiritual fulfillment. The Great Awakening and Holiness Movement in the United States revealed the deep spiritual need for something—Someone— more than the unholy modern trinity of "me, myself, and I." The movement away from self-sufficiency led to an acknowledgement that human existence is, at its very roots, reliant on God.

What are other historical or contemporary examples of the self-sufficient hero?

Why do you think our society elevates this kind of hero in popular culture?

Be Prepared for the Struggle

The counterpoint to the very basic human desire for protection is God's call for believers to be prepared. In the sixth chapter of his letter to the Ephesians, Paul challenges the Christians living in one of the largest and most diverse cities in Greece to not be discouraged by hostile opposition, but rather to take an aggressively peaceful response of preparation. The apostle encourages the young church to be "fitted with the readiness [*hetoimasia*] that comes with the gospel of peace" (Ephesians 6:15b). In other words, he tells them that in spite of the intense self-preservation instinct, the desire to turn and run away, they must be prepared to enter a dark world and stand with conviction for Jesus Christ.

Spiritual maturity is better understood as spiritual readiness: *Am I ready to enter the fray where my faith will be challenged and give my life completely into God's hands?* This is the kind of struggle that the apostle Paul lived out. Earlier in a letter to another church, the apostle reluctantly wrote to his detractors, "I have worked much harder, been in prison more frequently, been flogged more severely, and been exposed to death again and again. . . . Besides everything else, I face daily the pressure of my concern for all the churches" (2 Corinthians 11:23b-28). There was not a neutral zone for Christian believers then or now. Even Greek philosophers like Seneca recognized that life is a battle. And as Christians, we are called into the struggle.

Be prepared to enter a dark world and stand with conviction for Jesus Christ.

The apostle defines the struggle as "not against flesh and blood, but against . . . the powers of this dark world and against the spiritual forces of the heavenly realms" (Ephesians 6:12). The victory will not be easily won. The calling itself, however, is not to win, but to enter the conflict.

The apostle points out the real needs of those entering into the struggle:

- What we need is found *near* Christ. Christians do not seek security, but seek to "stand firm" with Him in the midst of life's struggles (Ephesians 6:13).

- What we need is found *with* Christ. Christians do not endure by their own strength, but "in the power of his might" (Ephesians 6:10, KJV).

- What we need is found *in only* Christ. Christians do not need protective charms and weapons, but instead, the defensive preparation of living in the Spirit as the "full armor of God," and the offensive tools of the "sword of the Spirit, which is the word of God" and "[prayer] in the Spirit on all occasions" (Ephesians 6:13, 17-18).

The messages of the following chapters will help flesh out the significance of the spiritual readiness to which all Christians are called:

The Real Enemy (Chapter 2): Our enemy is found in the spiritual powers and pervading darkness, not in "flesh and blood."

The Utility Belt of Truth (Chapter 3): The truth of the good news offers a heroic faith that is more powerful than any human can imagine.

The "Lorica" of Right Living (Chapter 4): The commitment to right living not only protects believers, but enables us to right the world's wrongs.

Walking on the Road to Peace (Chapter 5): The fitness of the disciple is found in his or her ability to carry the good news into hostile territory.

Delivered by the Helmet and Sword (Chapter 6): Salvation and the gospel are gifts of deliverance for both insiders and outsiders.

Prayer on Active Duty (Chapter 7): The missional life requires a willingness to enter into a life of active prayer for ourselves and others.

God's willingness to enter life's battle with us will be the focus in the following pages. The goal of this study will be joining Paul in "fearlessly [making] known the mystery of the gospel" (Ephesians 6:20). ●

Reflect on this...

What are the primary motives behind the desire for protection?

What is the significance of our battle being "not against flesh and blood"?

Where is spiritual conflict taking place? How do Christian believers know they are ready for the battle?

NOTES

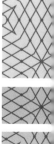

The Real Enemy

Fearful Folk Beliefs

Recently, my son attended a campout where he and others spent time sitting on logs in the glow of the campfire telling stories to make the spine tingle and skin crawl. The fear of darkness is nearly universal in human experience. Knowing there could be predators lurking just beyond the glow of the fire triggers a primordial instinct to be alert, to get ready to run for dear life. People have dealt with this fear in many ways throughout history. In the developed world today, the fear of darkness is not as pervasive since we can dismiss darkness with a flick of a light switch. Darkness for nearly half of each 24-hour day was a reality of human experience prior to the invention of electricity around 150 years ago. Before that, the fears of the darkness and its dangers were dealt with in another way.

Many cultures have believed (and some still believe) in the ability of an impersonal force to influence human endeavors. This force may work for good or ill, and may be manipulated by a knowledgeable person like a shaman who uses an object (talisman) or chant (mantra) to guide it. People in Melanesia call this spiritual force *mana*, but the concept is found around the world, from Native American to West African culture. The belief in a supernatural power at work in the natural world is also familiar in the modern, secular world—fans of the Star Wars films are familiar with the idea of an impersonal force manipulated by a few gifted people. This belief was also present in the first-century Roman Empire.

The Goddess of the Ancients

The great port city of Ephesus, located in present-day Turkey, was truly a crossroads of the Roman Empire. Near this grand, diverse city was the Temple of Artemis, one of the Seven Wonders of the (ancient) World. By the time of Paul's travels into the city, the cult of Artemis, (the Greek goddess of wisdom and fertility) spread through the city's population—Acts 19:23-41 records Paul's involvement in a riot led by artisans selling silver shrines to Artemis. This large statue of Artemis reflected the Ephesians' fears of the supernatural powers she represented.

The legends surrounding the Ephesian Artemis claimed the statue fell from the heavens (Acts 19:35). On her head she wore the crescent of the waxing moon, and she was said to preside over nighttime rituals at the temple. She was viewed as the supreme ruler of the heavenly realms, and wore a necklace containing all the planetary signs of the zodiac, which were believed to control the fates of all people. She was believed to provide success in the hunt with the bow and arrow she carried. She could bring illness as well as health, feed or bring sudden death; she ruled the heavens and the underworld. The people of Ephesus believed in her and feared her powers. For protection the people chanted the "Ephesian Grammata," six magical words spoken to bring one of her angels to aid them in a moment of trouble.

Reflect on this...

What are some contemporary forms of folk religion?

How seriously should Christians take the various forms of idolatrous worship in our world today?

How can Christians offer hope to those overwhelmed by fear and

uncertainty?

In this context, Paul arrived with the message of the good news. Later, in his letter to the Ephesians and other early Christians, he encouraged believers to "take [a] stand against the devil's schemes. . . . against the rulers, against the authorities, against the powers of this dark world and against the spiritual forces of evil in the heavenly realms" (Ephesians 6:11-12). Paul had already seen the hostility associated with the cult of Artemis in Ephesus (Acts 19) and acknowledged the presence of the "little gods" of folk religions that competed for attention and attempted to control peoples' hearts and minds.

The "Excluded Middle" of the Spiritual Conflict

The "excluded middle" of spiritual activity, according to former missionary and seminary professor Paul Hiebert, is neglected in today's emphasis on the supposed divide between the earthly and heavenly realms. Folk religions around the world recognize a god of birth, god of the planting, god of the hearth, god of the harvest, god of marriage, god of the forest, god of the river, and so on. From Paul's perspective as a Jewish rabbi, there was only one God: "Hear, O Israel: The LORD our God, the LORD is one" (Deuteronomy 6:4). Now, as a Christian missionary, Paul preached that the one God of Israel was fully revealed in the person of Jesus Christ and the power of the Holy Spirit (2 Corinthians 13:14). The "world rulers" (v. 12, *kosmocratoras*, a Greek word only found here) did not stand a chance against the one true God incarnated in Jesus of Nazareth. Because of Jesus, Paul had hope that victory was assured. Until then, the people of God needed more than protection—they needed to prepare for conflict.

The first step in preparing for the conflict is to realize that the struggle is not "against flesh and blood." (Ephesians 6:12). Historically, the church has been adept at identifying particular people as the primary foes of its work. The Spanish Inquisition, the papal polemic against Galileo, the Puritans' flight from Europe, and the witch trials of Salem testify to this fact. Today, the church continues to view certain politicians, filmmakers, and musicians as the primary aggressors against the gospel. But Paul knew better, and so should we. Paul had every right to be angry with the people of Ephesus, Damascus, Pisidian Antioch, Iconium, Philippi, and other places where he was beaten, arrested, or run out of town. Paul had a right to be angry when the Romans placed him on house arrest shackled to a Roman soldier, but he did not rail against the Emperor or the political system that jailed him. Paul knew that the spiritual battle extended far beyond the earthly realm, and sought to focus his readers on the spiritual task at hand.

Reflect on this...

What assurance does monotheism (belief in one God) offer Christian believers?

Think about ways Christians sometimes focus on "flesh-and-blood" enemies rather than the supernatural powers at work in the world.

The second step in preparing for the conflict is for believers to clothe themselves with Christlikeness. Three times in his letters to the Colossians and the Ephesians, Paul encourages Christians to "put on" the exterior virtues of their inner faith (Colossians 3:12; Ephesians 4:24, 6:11). In Ephesians 6, the clothing takes on the imagery of a warrior's armor (Greek, *panopolian*). The purpose of armor is not just to mimic full battle gear, but to show how the inner qualities of the heart must be evidenced in the believer's life. As Paul mentioned earlier in the letter, believers are to "be made new in the attitude of your minds; and to put on the new self, created to be like God in true righteousness and holiness" (4:23b-24). The world should be able to identify believers by how they live.

> The real call is to stand on the only solid foundation constructed of truth, righteousness, peace, faith, salvation, and the presence of the Spirit.

Paul states the third step in preparing for the conflict: "When the day of evil comes, you may be able to stand your ground, and after you have done everything, to stand. Stand firm . . ." (Ephesians 6:13b-14b). The three-fold repetition of the phrase "to stand" reveals the core task of the believer in a highly diverse and sometimes hostile context. Taking a stand does not mean adopting a my-way-or-the-highway approach when it comes to sharing our faith. Instead, Paul exhorts us to remain firm in our faith while reflecting Christ in our attitudes and actions. Taking a stand does not mean defeating our spiritual enemies with our own power—our true call is to stand on the solid foundation of truth, righteousness, peace, faith, salvation, and the presence of the Spirit. All other opposing forces, including idolatrous images, hatred, and unholy attitudes, will crumble while Christians stand firm in their convictions. While we stand, the darkness may surround us, but it will never overcome us, and in the end, we will know to whom we belong—and so will everyone else. ●

Reflect on this...

Is it difficult to imagine living the Christian life with all the attributes described by Paul in his letters to the Colossians and Ephesians (Colossians 3:12; Ephesians 4:23-34; Ephesians 6:11ff)?

What are some of your core convictions—the ones upon which you would take a stand?

3

The Utility Belt
of Truth

The Superhero's Essential Tool

Superheroes are known for their unique powers more than their costumes. Superman has the ability to fly and lift large objects, Spiderman the ability to spin a web and climb tall buildings, Wolverine the mutant ability to self-heal any wound, and the list continues. One popular hero from comic books and film, however, is not known for having superpowers—Batman. This character—the alter ego of billionaire Bruce Wayne—does not have the ability to fly, deflect bullets, spin webs or conjure superhuman strength. In spite of this apparent deficit, Batman has been battling villains, solving crimes, and protecting Gotham City since the character's introduction to the comic book world in 1939.

Batman is known for his crime-fighting gadgets. Much attention has been given in the film versions to the super-charged Batmobile, motorcycles, and flying machines. In the original comic book, his utility belt held as many as thirty items including a camera, two-way radio, handcuffs, smoke pellets, and the infamous batarangs (bat-shaped boomerangs that could take down any criminal). However, without his utility belt these inventive tools at Batman's disposal have limited usefulness.

In writing to the Ephesians about the "full armor of God," the first item on the list is the basic and most essential of all the qualities to be found among God's followers—the "belt of truth" (6:14). Other ancient sources give the essential tools of the Roman soldier, but it is interesting that Paul adds two obvious items not listed by others—the belt and footwear. These items are not limited to the soldier, but common among all people. These pieces of clothing provide protection from the ground in which one walks and provide a place to attach the tools needed for the work at hand. The notion of footwear will be covered in a later chapter, but here the significance of the belt will be the focus.

Reflect on this....

What superpowers would make it easier to be a Christian in today's world?

Who are the superheroes of faith in your own life?

What qualities make them heroic from your perspective?

Buckle Up to Stand Ready

The common use of the belt might easily dismiss it as something important. It is in fact the one item upon which everything else is attached. Its mundane usage in daily life also highlights a neglected aspect of its spiritual practicality for Christians who are believers in the "truth." The commitment to truth will provide Christian believers with the ability to stand in the face of internal and external conflict in their midst. They will not be caught off guard when the greatest challenges of one's time in history are encountered. The truth makes disciples ready to face whatever the enemy sends against them.

The phrase "gird up your loins" (ASV, ERV) is used by Paul in verse 14 to signify the need for being alert and ready when the battle comes. In Jeremiah, the first chapter, Yahweh calls the young man to be His spokesperson, to speak to the disobedient nation: "Get yourself ready! [gird yourself] Stand up and say to them whatever I command" (1:17). In 1 Peter 1:13 similar language is used again by Paul's compatriot to encourage disciples to be alert and ready "with minds that are alert [minds girded up] and fully sober." Paul called believers to have "buckled around your waist [girded about the loins]" the very "belt of truth," the essence of what holds up the Christian life. These verses allude to several tools which are attached to the belt of truth enabling the Christian to stand firm in the face of opposition.

> The commitment to truth will provide Christian believers with the ability to stand in the face of internal and external conflict in their midst.

The Usefulness of the Belt of Truth

Trust the Commander's voice. Commentators have compared Ephesians 6 to a military speech, much like a rousing pep talk just prior to battle. To move into the line of fire, the troops need to trust their commanding officer in order to obey the commands and not their survival instinct to run toward safety. God's command comes to His people, but He offers a way through Jesus Christ to listen to His people—it's a two-way radio hanging on the belt of truth. God's blessings are the bestowal of the gifts and graces needed to stand firm for Him. Paul begins the letter to Ephesians in praise to the "God and Father of our Lord Jesus Christ, who has blessed us in the heavenly realms with every spiritual blessing in Christ" (1:3). There is no reason to not trust in the God who calls us to bring light into a darkened and hostile world. Will we trust our instincts or the voice of the Commander? In Paul's words written in another letter, "The one who calls you is faithful, and he will do it" (1 Thessalonians 5:24).

Live in the reality of faithful obedience. First century Roman society teemed with prevalent "mystery religions" that offered secrets to healthy and wealthy lives by entering into shadowy cultic practices, much like today's secret societies. These religions promised an antidote to the fear of the unknown and the certainty of death. To find one's destiny was the goal, and it came with a steep price, usually expensive participation in elaborate rituals that separated one from family and work responsibilities. The hook for these mysteries was the hidden secret that held captive its supposed truth. The alternative offered by the Christian faith was not to be found in the shadow of darkness but in the "fruit of the light," which "consists in all goodness, righteousness and truth" (Ephesians 4:25). The Christian is prepared to battle in the darkness by being the light.

Reflect on this...

In what ways is the Commander's voice drowned out by distractions from the world?

What are some examples of "secret knowledge" that are promised by leading thought in today's world? How susceptible are Christians to seek this hidden knowledge?

Rely not on human efforts but on God's truth. Besides mystery religions, there were prominent philosophical movements abounding in Paul's day that garnered support from all corners. Paul exemplified an acute awareness of these movements that included the Stoics, Cynics, and Epicureans, especially in his sermons recorded in the book of Acts (especially chapters 14 and 17). These philosophical societies taught that people should put required personal attributes of reason, virtue, and wise speech, using the same imagery of armor for battle. Seneca, the great Stoic philosopher, is known to have stated that "life is a battle." The armor for the ancient philosophers was the result of human effort and self-reliance. Paul borrows the concept but changes the imagery. Rather than human ingenuity, the apostle calls believers to take on the qualities that result from trust in God—right living, peace, readiness, and reliance upon His Word. The preparation of the disciple is geared toward the truth of the good news found once and for all in the person of Jesus Christ.

The Truth of the Good News for Less-than-Superheroes of Faith

The good news offers truth that transcends the popular religious notions and the common mindset of the day. Paul offered one of the earliest synopsis of the gospel message in the first letter to the Corinthian church:

> "For what I received I passed on to you as of first importance: that Christ died for our sins according to the Scriptures, that he was buried, that he was raised on the third day according to the Scriptures, and that he appeared to Cephas, and then to the Twelve" (15:3-5).

The good news brings hope to the living: *Jesus lived on earth as an example of holy living.* The good news brings hope to the sinful and despondent: *Jesus died to bring salvation to all who believe in Him.* The gospel brings hope to those living in bondage to the sinful social structures of this world: *Christ is risen again, and His new life will overcome the ways of the world leading to defeat and despondency.* There is one other aspect of the good news: *Jesus appeared to His disciples after His resurrection and ascended from earth to heaven to be at the right hand of the Father.* Jesus Christ is not just Lord of the earth but of all the heavens. Christ is the Victor on a cosmic scale. Jesus lived on earth to show us an alternative way to live in this world, defeated death, and now extends the power of the Most High God over any rivals. It is upon this truth that the Christian enters the frayed, pluralistic world to do battle not against "flesh and blood" but against darkness itself through believers known now as "children of light" (Ephesians 5:9; 6:12). For this task, Christians do not need access to superpowers, just access to the essentials of faith found in the utility "belt of truth." ●

Reflect on this...

When have you sought to do work for God through your own efforts?

What lessons did you learn that taught you to trust in God alone?

What does it mean to wear the belt of truth in your own life?

NOTES:

The "Lorica" of Right Living

Patrick's Lorica

There is a legend surrounding the life of Patrick, patron saint of Ireland. It is said that Patrick was traveling a lonely road through an Irish forest with his small band of missionary priests. A local chieftain known for his hostility toward Patrick, and everything else that was true to the Christian God, sent warriors to dispatch the missionaries into the eternity they spoke of so often. Patrick began to sing a prayer that changed himself and the other missionaries into a bevy of red deer. The chieftain's men bumbled past the disguised missionaries, ignoring the deer off to the side of the path. Since then, the lines of this song are used as a prayer of protection, particularly at the beginning of the day or a long journey. The song is known as "St Patrick's Lorica," literally, "the breastplate of Patrick."

A cursory reading of St. Patrick's Lorica will show that the words point to a much more powerful reality than the quaint, fairy-tale feel of the legendary story associated with it. The song invokes the Trinity—Father, Son, and Holy Spirit—for guidance and protection for a new day. The song recounts the gospel story of Jesus, the heritage of faith arising from the prophets and apostles, and the incitement to faith in God from the witness of all creation. The prayer asks for protection from the many inner temptations and outward obstacles that so easily trap the faithful. The climax of the song comes in the second to last stanza:

Christ be with me, Christ within me,
Christ behind me, Christ before me,
Christ beside me, Christ to win me,
Christ to comfort and restore me.
Christ beneath me, Christ above me,
Christ in quiet, Christ in danger,
Christ in hearts of all that love me,
Christ in mouth of friend and stranger.

The importance of this prayer is not the stuff of magical fairy tales. Instead, the words attributed to the 5th century missionary priest acknowledge the reality that the Christian believers' protection comes from an active faith engaged in every aspect of life.

Reflect on this...

What aspects of this prayer would have helped you begin a day from the previous week?

Why is it sometimes easier to believe a legend than the true stories of regular life?

In what obstacles or difficulties have you needed God's direct intervention?

Making Things Right

The sixth chapter of Ephesians introduces the full armor of God, including the "breastplate of righteousness." Here the apostle cites the Hebrew prophet Isaiah. In it there is a lament that "justice is far from us, and righteousness

does not overtake us; we hope for light, but behold, darkness" (59:9).
Everyone was turning away from Yahweh and the true path of life-giving
covenant He made with His people. "It was displeasing in his sight that there
was no justice" (v. 15b). It is at this point God takes it upon himself to make a
way of redemption for His people putting on "righteousness like a breastplate"
(v. 17), and correcting the wrongs, bringing judgment upon the disobedient,
and renewing His covenant with His people. The covenant is to be founded
on justice: living rightly in a world gone all wrong.

Righteousness is both a gift and an act. Paul describes righteousness as a
gift—"God's abundant provision of grace" (Romans 5:17). To be made right is
the result of God's masterful hand in shaping a life given fully to Him. There
is nothing Christians can do to prepare for what God does in their lives any
more than a lump of clay can envision the beautiful vessel it will become in
the potter's workshop. As we enter more fully into God's presence, the shape
of God's workmanship should become obvious in how the vessel is used. Will
it be used to the fullness of its functionality? Or will its potential remain
latent? The answers to these questions come through comprehending that the
artisan's attributes should be seen through the vessel in its qualities and its
functions. Does it do what the Creator intended?

The character of God will always leave traces of His creative presence upon
the lives He reshapes. In this way, Christians will see God's character in
their lives much like artisans leave signatures on a piece of their work. The
righteous life is the result of God's work but it is completed through the lives
of God's followers.

Reflect on this...

Read through Isaiah 59 and identify how God wants to make right the wrongs in the world and in the human heart?

Why is it important to remember that righteousness is both a gift and an action?

What encouragement can you take from having God's signature placed upon your heart and life?

The Blood and the Breath of Christian Vitality

The method God uses to shape human lives can be seen in the parts of the body that the breastplate of righteousness is meant to protect. Metal or leather is strapped to the torso to cover the heart and lungs. The source of life within the body is the blood. It transports life-giving nutrients to the rest of the body. The heart moves this essential fluid. Any organ, no matter how central to the functioning of the body, will not exist for very long without the blood. The blood needs to be infused with oxygen to bring what is needed to each organ. The lungs convert oxygen from the air breathed into the blood enriching the body. The blood and breath enliven the lump of carbon-based "dust" of the human body. In a similar way, it is the spiritual blood and breath that become the impetus for righteousness living—both the blood of the Word and the breath of the Spirit at work in human lives.

> **Being a Christian with a purpose is to be Christian on purpose.**

Christian vitality is not simply having access to the best option in the marketplace of ideas (right teaching) or being fully-mature and emotionally well-balanced (right attitude). Vitality is found as it is expressed in how believers live daily (right actions). Theologians call this "orthopraxy" (some Christian leaders call it social justice). In the French language, the word for righteousness is simply "justice." To be just is to be righteous, and to live justly will mean being righteous. Christians cannot call themselves inwardly righteous and act outwardly in ways that tilt the balance of justice in opposition to God's character. The function of the vessel will then no longer reflect the attributes of the Creator. The vessel's function will be counterproductive to its original design. The intent of the artisan will be lost. Returning to Isaiah's word against the disobedient, the prophet wrote, "According to their deeds, so He will repay, wrath to His adversaries, and recompense to His enemies" (59:18).

The key issue in what it means to live righteously in the world is found in intentionality. Being a Christian with *a* purpose is to be Christian *on* purpose. When injustice shows its ugly face to the world, the Christian is to stand in opposition. This will be a dangerous position for it will most certainly be unpopular to those of influence and power. This is the very reason of putting on the armor: to be prepared to make a stand when necessary. The life of Jesus gives a clue as to when His followers are to take a stance.

how would I my relationships as :
areas where I struggle to live right are :
I need God to help me in my life by :

Quoting the prophet Isaiah, Jesus read the following in the synagogue of His hometown Nazareth:

"The Spirit of the Lord is on me, because he has anointed me to proclaim good news to the poor. He has sent me to proclaim freedom for the prisoners and recovery of sight for the blind, to set the oppressed free, to proclaim the year of the Lord's favor" (Luke 4:18-19; Isaiah 61:1-2; 58:6).

These were not only words to exemplify the character of Jesus in the world, it is also the calling of His disciples. These behaviors become the signature of authenticity in the way Christians live. ●

Reflect on this...

What is the significance of justice in the Christian life? In the church? In the individual?

Why is it difficult to take a stand to make right the wrongs of the world?

What hope can we gain from the life of Jesus on earth?

NOTES:

5

Walking on the Road to Peace

The Road to Peace

Shoes are apparently a hot commodity these days. A well-known shoe designer recently created a pair of diamond-encrusted women's dress pumps that cost over $400,000. The workshop where these shoes were made required numerous security guards. The effort required making these shoes could only be attributed to the garish affluence in which even more is never enough. On the other hand, the sale of the shoe raised nearly $500,000 for a charity auction. For the less wealthy, some shoes worn by well-known athletic stars can sell for thousands of dollars. Although many people today are less inclined toward such well-endowed shoes, the importance of footwear is not lost on those of the ancient world.

The Roman Empire expanded by the influence and strength of its military superiority. Its soldiers were well-equipped to endure long marches in a wide range of climates, from the arid deserts of northern Africa to the soggy moss lands of present-day Scotland. In fact, the foundation walls of an ancient Roman military fort dating from AD 165 were discovered in 2011 at the construction site of a supermarket north of Glasgow. In the midst of these ancient walls was a cache of several dozen hobnailed military sandals in very good condition. The Roman soldiers' sandals trod hundreds of miles in service of the imperial army. Compared to today's shoes, the footwear was not much, being made of a fitted scrap of leather held tight by leather straps with metal nobs, providing limited traction. In the days of the first century, however, most sandals carried the imperial message to distant lands that a new power was in place, and its footing was secure. It was into this context Paul carried a new message—not of imperial might but of spiritual power.

The feet of the early disciples were able to cross vast distances, especially from the perspective of the first century, due to the system of paved roads crisscrossing the ancient imperial territory, totaling 50,000 miles from Africa, Western Europe, and north into Britain. Some of these roads offered a passage way that still exists underneath modern-day motorways. In Paul's day, the most prominent way to travel these roads was by foot. These feet were to bring a message of peace found only in the gospel of Jesus Christ. The apostle Paul logged nearly 7,000 miles on his three missionary journeys recorded in the book of Acts. He was no stranger of the road.

Reflect on this...

Describe an outdoor activity for which you were not properly dressed. What went wrong?

In what ways are you surprised about the distances traveled in the ancient world?

What else do you know about the Roman Empire that allowed Paul to travel so widely and speak so freely?

Not According to Plan

In his letter to the Romans, Paul asks, "And how can anyone preach unless they are sent?" He then paraphrases Isaiah by adding this quote, "How beautiful are the feet of those who bring good news!" (Romans 10:15; see Isaiah 52:7). In Ephesians 6, the apostle offers a list of the "full armor of God," including "feet fitted with the readiness that comes from the gospel of peace" (v. 15). The emphasis for Paul is not on the type of footwear needed by the disciples but the quality of the feet in preparation for the task ahead. The followers of Jesus were to bring the "gospel of peace" into a divisive, hostile, and sometimes violent world. The quality of the messenger needs to align with the message. In Romans 10:15, the reference to "beautiful feet" does not mean good looking or well-pedicured toes and heels. Rather, the idea is that the feet will radiate moral beauty, a satisfaction that comes from being made whole—the "peace" that comes with the gospel. These messengers should be recognized as Christian disciples since they bring with them a message of goodness and justice into the places they travel.

This was the plan, and the plan did not always work as expected. On Paul's first missionary journey, he and Barnabas traveled far from the paved roads of the empire into Lystra (Acts 14). The people had mistaken the missionaries as demigods in disguise, the offspring of Greek gods and humans, in the same vein as the legendary myths of Hercules. Barnabas, the elder of the two, was taken for Zeus, and Paul the outspoken one, was considered to be Hermes, the messenger between the gods and humans. The local people attempted to make sacrifices to them as divine entities. Paul tried to admonish them by saying, "We are bringing you good news, telling you to turn from these worthless things to the living God" (v. 16). The people still tried to sacrifice to them until the crowds were convinced by legalistic Jewish extremists that Paul and Barnabas were imposters. Paul was stoned by the people and left for dead. The gospel of peace was not always received with open arms but sometimes with a clinched fist.

The hostile response to the good news did not refute the message. The strength of the good news is not in the written or spoken words of the message but within the words of Jesus Christ. It was not knowledge of Israel's laws or being foreign to the covenant that mattered. Paul's letter to Ephesians makes this clear, "For he himself is our peace, who has made the two groups one and has destroyed the barrier the dividing wall of hostility" (2:14). Jesus Christ entered the world "to reconcile both of them to God through the cross, by which he put to death hostility" (v. 16). Rather, Jesus brought the message of "peace to you who were far away and peace to those who were near" (v. 17). It no longer matters whether one is a religious insider or skeptical outsider, Christ's death and resurrection brings reconciliation through new life in Him.

Reflect on this...

Why is the quality of the messenger so essential to understand and receive the message they bring?

What are the qualities mentioned in the Scripture passages of this chapter that illustrate the kind of messenger God is looking for?

How is Jesus the ideal messenger for the gospel of peace?

Protection from the Enemy's Verbal Barrage

The feet bringing peace were to be accompanied by the protective armament of the "shield of faith" (Ephesians 6:16). The shield in this passage is not the small, lightweight shield known as an *aspis*, but the larger one known as the *thyreos*. This five-foot high shield protected the entire body. It was usually made of wood and covered in animal leather. The covering was soaked in water to protect flaming arrows of the enemy launched from a distance. The shield symbolizes both the nature of the enemy's attack and the type of protection that the disciple is given in relationship with God.

> **The protection of the shield is found in the faithfulness and trustworthiness of God's incarnate word Jesus Christ.**

The "burning arrows" may be construed as the insinuations of evil speech. In Proverbs 26:18, it is written: "Like a maniac shooting flaming arrows of death is one who deceives their neighbor . . ." The deceptive speech between neighbors is amplified by hostility and fed by wickedness. The first verse of Psalms mentions the cancerous growth of sinful speech. Notice the progression in this passage: "Blessed is the one who does not walk in step with the wicked or stand in the way that sinners take or sit in the company of mockers . . ." (1:1). Those that walk in wickedness, stand with sinners, and then sit in the midst of those mocking the faith of God's followers. Protection from the enemy's onslaught is not simply to watch one's language or to speak in relevant and convincing words. The protection of the shield is found in the faithfulness and trustworthiness of God's incarnate word Jesus Christ.

The irony of the armor of God is that the implements associated with competition, violence, and war are used by the apostle to illustrate how to bring about peace among all people. The people of God are sent into the center of the hostile and violent clashes between the enemy and the hearts and minds of those he is attempting to conquer. The major obstacle to the enemy's methods is the "complete unity" found among the disciples of Christ. It is living in the faithfulness of God in the peace given only by Him that in the words of Jesus' prayer to the Father become true, so that "the world will know that you sent me and have loved them even as you have loved me" (John 17:23). ●

Reflect on this...

What do the "burning arrows" say about the kinds of attacks brought by the enemy?

Why do you think words are so powerful?

What do you think about the Paul's usage of military armor to illustrate Christian virtues?

NOTES:

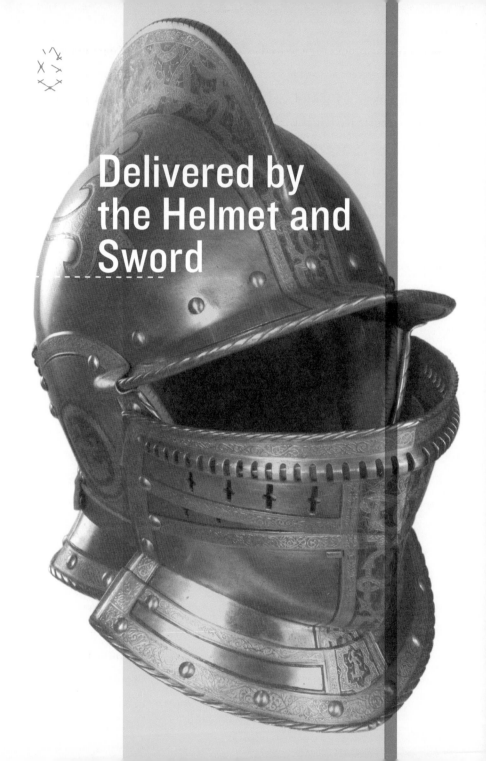

Delivered by the Helmet and Sword

Salvation is sometimes characterized as a decision to act upon God's grace. An unbeliever moves forward to kneel at an altar, prays a simple prayer, and raises one's hand in acknowledgement of God's saving grace. This is obviously an aspect of the divine initiative that calls for a human response. In many cases, the emphasis on decision overshadows all that has already happened in God's saving action. The two remaining objects in the "full armor of God" are gifts that are not to be received by the committed disciple: "Take the helmet of salvation and the sword of the Spirit, which is the word of God" (Ephesians 6:17). The people of God cannot arm themselves, they are to rely on what only God can give.

Salvation as the Gift of Deliverance

The apostle Paul draws on imagery already found in Isaiah's writings: God "put on righteousness as His breastplate, and the helmet of salvation on his head; he put on the garments of vengeance and wrapped himself in zeal as in a cloak" (59:17). Salvation is God's intervention into the messiness of human lives. God is more like a rescue worker entering the fiery building or jumping into the murky waters to pull the unbeliever to safety in His arms. God wants to deliver His people from the bondage of "the powers of this dark world" and "the spiritual forces of evil in the heavenly realms" (Ephesians 6:13). In other words, God is not asking His people to do what He has not already done. God wants us to join Him in offering the gift of His helmet of salvation— His deliverance—to all people.

Salvation is a gift, but what exactly does this mean? The book of Genesis offers a glimpse at just how God goes about saving His people. Noah is commanded to build a boat to save a remnant of people and animals. They are chosen by God for the purpose of starting all over again. Up to this point the human race was only good at being "only evil all the time"

(Genesis 6:5). The Lord even "regretted" creating the human race (verse 6). Chapter seven contains a complete reversal of the creation account of the first chapter: the chaotic waters (symbolizing evil and the ungodly) overtook the mountains, the birds, animals, swarming animals and humankind, except for Noah's remnant. There is a reboot of the original command of God upon His creation: go and multiply (Genesis 8:17; 1:29). They were saved for the purpose of starting again.

Reflect on this...

What kind of significance does it make to realize salvation as a gift?

What other images besides deliverance come to mind when describing God's gift of salvation?

Abraham received a calling for the purpose of fulfilling God's command to multiply in order to bless every nation through one family. It was by no means an easy journey for Abraham and his family. In fact God worked around the continual unfaithfulness of Abraham's descendants, such as the trickery of Jacob and the jealousy of his sons. It was not until Joseph, the son left for dead by his brothers, was able to bring about a blessing to other nations as he did in service to Egypt. Jacob's family—God's chosen people—was saved from a famine by Joseph so that Jacob could become the blessing it was meant to be. Conversely, once several generations passed by in Egypt, God's people were in need of being saved from being enslaved laborers. Moses, left for dead along the Nile, was raised in the Pharaoh's household to a position of authority. In a swift turn of events, he had to flee in fear and disgrace, only to return at God's heeding to lead His people to freedom in the wilderness. God's people were saved from what they were in order to become what God wanted them to be.

> **The Spirit will empower the Message to vanquish the dark forces attempting to hold the world captive.**

In each case salvation from God meant deliverance for His people. Noah, Abraham, Jacob and Moses were required to leave what was familiar and venture into the unknown. They did not have a certain path before them, only a trustworthy voice guiding them. Salvation was truly a gift that was received, sometimes in spite of their inability to recognize what God was doing in their lives. The gift of salvation—to be delivered from sin and toward life in Christ—has been given, but it must also be received.

Reflect on this...

In what ways does today's church life emphasize the importance of the human aspect of "making a decision"?

What are some reminders from your own walk with God about how He was at work in you before you decided to follow Him?

When you consider your walk with God, how was God's delivering presence first made obvious to you?

The Sword of the Spirit

The imagery of the "sword of the Spirit" uses a particular word for the short sword used in close combat. The only offensive weapon given in the armament of God's people is not to be launched from a safe distance. It is only in the context of close contact with the darkness that God's people will make their stand for what is good, right, and holy. It is not the sword alone that will convince the world. Here the sword is the gospel message, literally, *rhema* in Greek as in "*Word* of God." Rather, it is the "sword" empowered by "the Spirit." The Spirit will empower the Message to vanquish the dark forces attempting to hold the world captive.

The gospel message is compared to a sword in several places in the Bible. Isaiah proves once again to be the source for Paul's thoughts: "He will strike the earth with the rod of his mouth; with the breath of his lips he will slay the wicked" (11:4). This verse provides the context for Paul elsewhere on the sword being a weapon of judgment against evil in the last days (2 Thessalonians 2:8). There is also an application in the daily life of the disciple in that the gospel ("Word of God") is "alive and active. Sharper than any double-edged sword . . . it judges the thoughts and attitudes of the heart" (Hebrews 4:12). The Word of God can do so, Paul writes, "because our gospel came to you not simply with words but also with power, with the Holy Spirit and deep conviction" (1 Thessalonians 1:5). The imagery of the sword of the Spirit as a tool of judgment guiding His people toward repentance is prevalent in Revelation (1:16; 2:12, 16; 19:13-15).

> No one has an inside track to God's salvation—all are in need of grace.

The Word of God as the "gospel of peace" (mentioned in verse 15) is the corrective needed to defeat the enemy. The alienating powers of darkness separate people from each other and from God. The hostility of this world will only be overturned as God's presence is made known, and this is accomplished by God's people. There is no difference in God's word to Abraham long ago, and what God has in store for His people today, that "all peoples on earth will be blessed through you" (Genesis 12:3). The power of salvation is not to conquer other nations but to heal the wounds, bring together divided peoples, and announce the gospel "because it is the power of God that brings salvation to everyone who believes" (Romans 1:12). It is important to read the rest of verse 12: "first to the Jew, then to the Gentile." Salvation is for all who believe—those that are spiritual insiders, recipients of the first covenant, and the spiritual outsiders, the ones living in alienation from God. No one has an inside track to God's salvation—all are in need of grace. In Paul's words, "this is not from yourselves, it is the gift of God—not by works, so that no one can boast" (Ephesians 2:8-9). ●

Reflect on this...

In what ways does the gospel bring judgment upon the world, and how do we reconcile this with being "good news" and the "gospel of peace"?

How would you define grace to someone unfamiliar with spiritual things?

Why do you think the images of "helmet" and "sword" are used by Paul to describe salvation and the gospel, respectively?

NOTES:

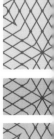

7

Prayer on Active Duty

Ephesians 6 is about being prepared as a disciple to live in a world darkened by hostility. The call to preparation includes putting on the "full armor of God." One piece of armor will not do. It is not enough to be partially prepared, but to be fully ready to enter into the fray. Christian disciples are to be God's envoys just as rays of sunlight cut through the shadows. The full force of this passage is in the apostle's encouragement to "stand firm" (v. 14). This imperative command is repeated three times and provides an anchor for the other actions found in the passage: to buckle up the belt of truth and breastplate of righteousness, to fit one's feet with the gospel of peace, and to take up the shield of faith" (vv. 14-16). Once fitted with the armor, the helmet of salvation and sword of the Spirit, meaning the gospel are to be received as the final preparation for the coming battle against evil. Once prepared, however, the Christian must enter the struggle.

Prayer is the central action of the Christian soldier. The military imagery is again subverted by a counterpoint. The Christian does not need greater power, more equipment, or enough time. The Christian "soldier" is not one typically found in a great army. The disciple's strength is found in the attitude of the heart and inclination toward active prayer. The Christian to be fully prepared must simply seek the Lord by speaking with Him. The passage does not simply offer the encouragement to pray but gives some clues as to how to do so.

> ## Prayer is the central action of the Christian soldier.

The Christian prays only with the Spirit's help. Paul's encouragement to "pray in the Spirit" is reminiscent of his words to the Romans. There Paul describes the person "led by the Spirit God" (8:14ff), and the ways the Spirit helps believers into conversations with the very "mind of the Spirit" as He "searches our hearts" and "intercedes for us" when one does not know exactly how to pray or what words to use. (vv. 26-27). The assistance of the Spirit leaves no room for excuse or lack of practice. The Spirit helps us to know Him more. There is no novice in the school of prayer. The Greek word for "all" is found four times in verse 18: "all occasions . . . all kinds of prayers. . . . always keep on praying . . . for all the Lord's people." At each point, the Spirit is there to help Christians pray.

The Christian is to be continually in prayer. The life of prayer is not to bookend each day but a way of living every moment in God's presence. Paul already encouraged the church to "pray continually" (1 Thessalonians 5:17), and now the apostle gives further instruction. There is no occasion when prayer is not an appropriate response. Prayer can be simply taking on a continual inclination toward God in all things. Is God the first direction one turns for guidance? God is more readily accessible and more reliable than Google—do we really believe this today? Prayer can also be the articulation of specific requests to Him; there is no request too mundane or insignificant for God. To pray continually is to always be alert, to stand ready for the opportunity to follow God wherever He leads, and to respond in Christlike obedience (Luke 21:36).

The Christian is to ask for prayer as well as to pray for others. In the midst of the apostle's encouragement for disciples to pray for all of God's people, Paul also asks for prayer. No Christian, not even Paul, the author of 60% of the New Testament, is beyond the need for prayer. The willingness to pray for others, and be prayed for by others, shows the apostle's complete trust in someone other than himself. The contemporary mindset is very much one of self-reliance but Paul has no room for this attitude. To let go of the reins of our lives is to turn our faces toward God, and trust in Him alone. Prayer is the primary way to let go by letting Him work in our lives and into the world through us. The assurance for the Christian is the knowledge that the Spirit is always with us.

Reflect on this...

What times can you recall when the Spirit had to intercede on your behalf when words failed you?

Which aspect of prayer for you is most difficult: maintaining an attitude of prayer or bringing specific requests to Him?

Why do you think it is difficult for some people to ask for prayer?

The Christian prays in order to speak of the gospel without inhibition. The power of prayer emboldens believers to open up their hearts toward God and to open their mouths about Him. Paul asks for the boldness to speak "fearlessly" (Ephesians 6:19). Reputations and good intentions are no match for speaking freely of the gospel. This is not an excuse to be a societal irritant. Christians that only speak in religious overtones and spiritual clichés can be quickly dismissed by others as ignorant and boorish. Rather,

Christian disciples should be able to converse in every subject imaginable, but with humility. Paul's intention is that when Christians are faced by intense hostility they have the fearlessness to speak God's truth in a way that exudes Christlikeness. The reception will not always be joyful, and there may be social repercussions. The Christian should not be tempted to follow the continually changing voices of public opinion (Ephesians 4:14). The responsibility of the Christian is to personify the gospel message by "speaking the truth in love" (v.15).

All Kinds of Active Prayer

Prayer is an attitude, an inclination toward obedience of talking to and hearing from God. Prayer is also an activity. There are various ways to practice prayer. Adele Ahlberg Calhoun offers several suggestions about how Christians can enter into a life of prayer (*Spiritual Disciplines Handbook*, IVP Books, 2005).

Fixed-hour Prayer. Long ago Benedict created a schedule of work and prayer for monks in his monastery. Eight times per day the monks gathered for prayer: in the middle of the night, in waking up, before beginning work, at mid-morning, at noon, at mid-afternoon, in the evening, and just before sleep. Many of us live by our daily calendar and to-do lists so nothing is left out or forgotten. Why wouldn't we do the same for prayer? Even if this regulated approach seems daunting, try two or three of the times. Or, take the restless sleep in the middle of the night and turn it into a sacred time of prayer.

Prayer Walk. This is a type of intercessory prayer. The emphasis and content of the prayer is specific and contextual. I know a man in Philadelphia that walked his drug-infested neighborhood for ten years, praying for homes, families, and even for the drug dealers on the corners. Today the neighborhood is revitalized, people have been saved, the drug dealers are fewer, and the effectiveness of prayer is obvious to all living there.

Scriptural Prayers. One of the greatest textbooks for prayer in the whole world is found in the Bible. The Psalms offer very human words as a way of exalting and lamenting life with God. Make the Psalms a personal prayer by putting your name in place of the personal pronouns "I," "me," and "us." Calhoun suggests trying this with Psalm 139:13-14. The New Testament has several written prayers that can be personalized as a word of prayer, notably Ephesians 1:3-14 and 1 Peter 1:3-9.

Praying the Hymns. This practice is related to scriptural prayer. I have taken the grand hymns of the faith and spoken them as prayers. Instead of singing them with the familiar melodies, I have read them aloud according to the written punctuation. The intense meaning of "O Great Thou Art" and "Be Thou My Vision" become a spoken path to deeper communion with God.

Contemplative Prayer. There is a misconception that contemplation equals mindlessness. This is exactly the opposite of what has been practiced in Christian traditions. Contemplation is simply giving all one's attention toward God's presence, and allowing Him to speak into one's life. The practice usually is aided by focusing on a specific verse of scripture or line from a hymn. The intense focus on these brief phrases offer a portal into what God intends for His people.

Prayer Partners. Conversations with God are not an individualized act. Joining with another person in praying is really the ideal context for prayer (Matthew 18:20). Celtic Christians spoke often of finding one's *anam cara* (soul friend). In popular culture, this notion is usually infused with romantic overtones using the phrase "soul mate." This is not the original intent, but rather it means spiritual friendship. By coming together in spiritual friendship the human interaction of conversation corresponds to the deep relational connection found in the Trinity. Prayer becomes the primary means of relating to God and others. ●

Reflect on this...

Describe times when you have prayed through the scriptures or through the hymnal.

Why is it important to pray with others?

Why do you think prayer is so crucial to the Christian life?

NOTES:

NOTES:

Other Dialog studies also available!

FAITH AMONG FRIENDS
Creating Intentional Conversations

How should people of faith live among the unfaithful? How will non-Christians see the love of God in our lives? *Faith Among Friends* reveals the many ways our lives as Christians testify to who the Lord is, what he has to say, and how he can change lives.

PARTICIPANT'S GUIDE ISBN: 978-0-8341-3139-2
FACILITATOR'S GUIDE ISBN: 978-0-8341-3140-8

REVELATION
Exploring God's Redemptive Plan

The mention of the book of Revelation conjures so many images of doom and gloom that we often miss the point. *Revelation* looks beyond the "end-of-days" scenarios to help you understand its place in the arc of Scripture and how it reveals salvation for humankind.

PARTICIPANT'S GUIDE ISBN: 978-0-8341-3143-9
FACILITATOR'S GUIDE ISBN: 978-0-8341-3144-6

Available online at DialogSeries.com